Dot to Dot Animals and Nature Book for Adults
Puzzles from 334 to 654 Dots

By Laura's Dot to Dot Therapy

How To Use This Book

Hi! We're so glad you're a lover of puzzles and dot connecting- we are too!

Connecting the dots in this book is simple- just relax and follow the numbers in consecutive order, drawing a straight line between each one. Dot 1 will connect to dot 2 and so on and so forth until there are no more dots to connect. There's always another dot and you'll always find it. Connect every dot to discover the beautiful images they create.

In case you get lost or can't find a dot, never stress- there's an answer key at the back of the book that will show you exactly where each dot connects to the next. If you want to color your images, we encourage you to do so! Feel free to try all different colors and coloring mediums for your images!

If you find any errors or omissions in this book, email us at Laurasdottodot@gmail.com and please let us know! We want you to have the best dot to dot experience!

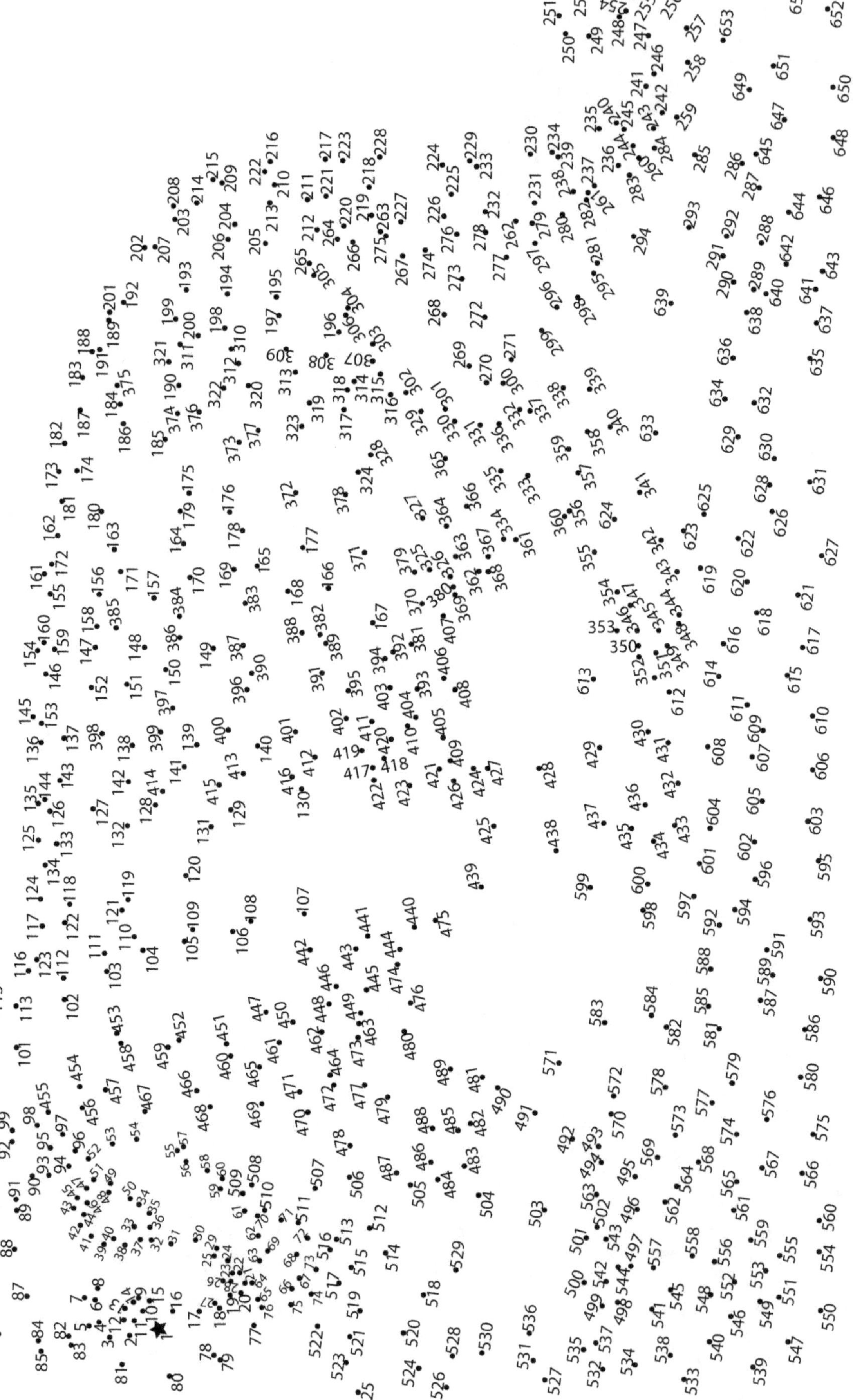

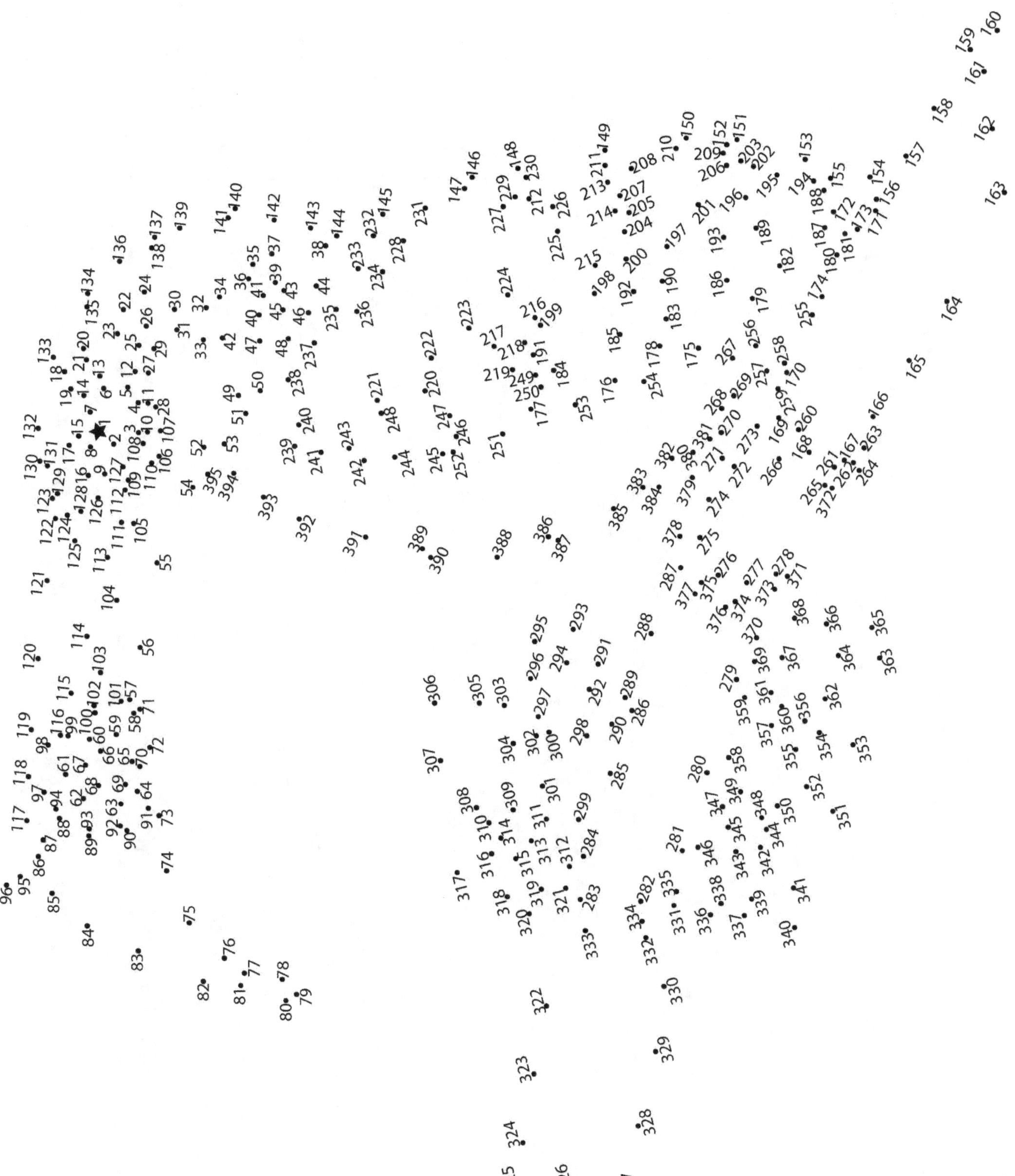

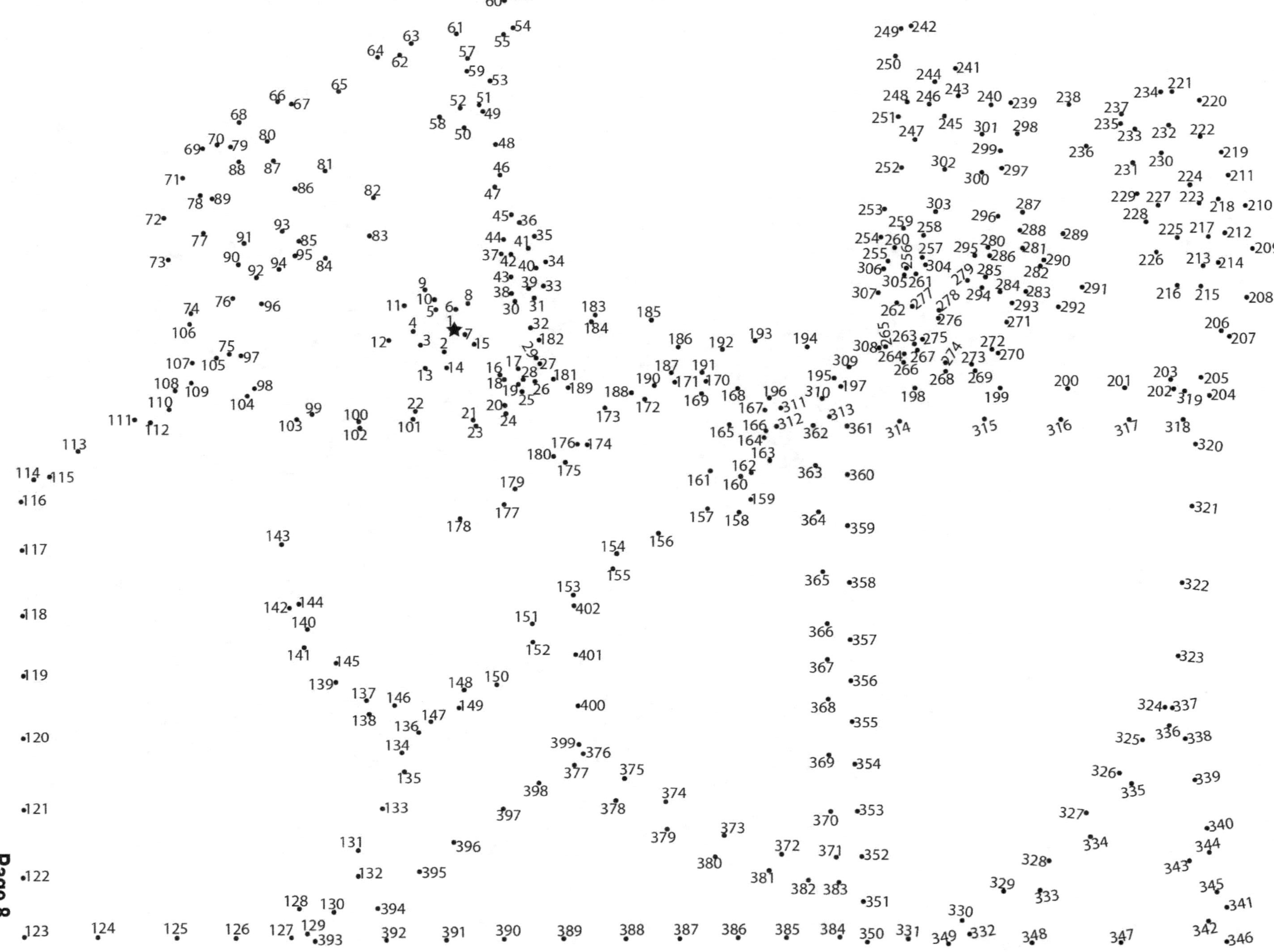

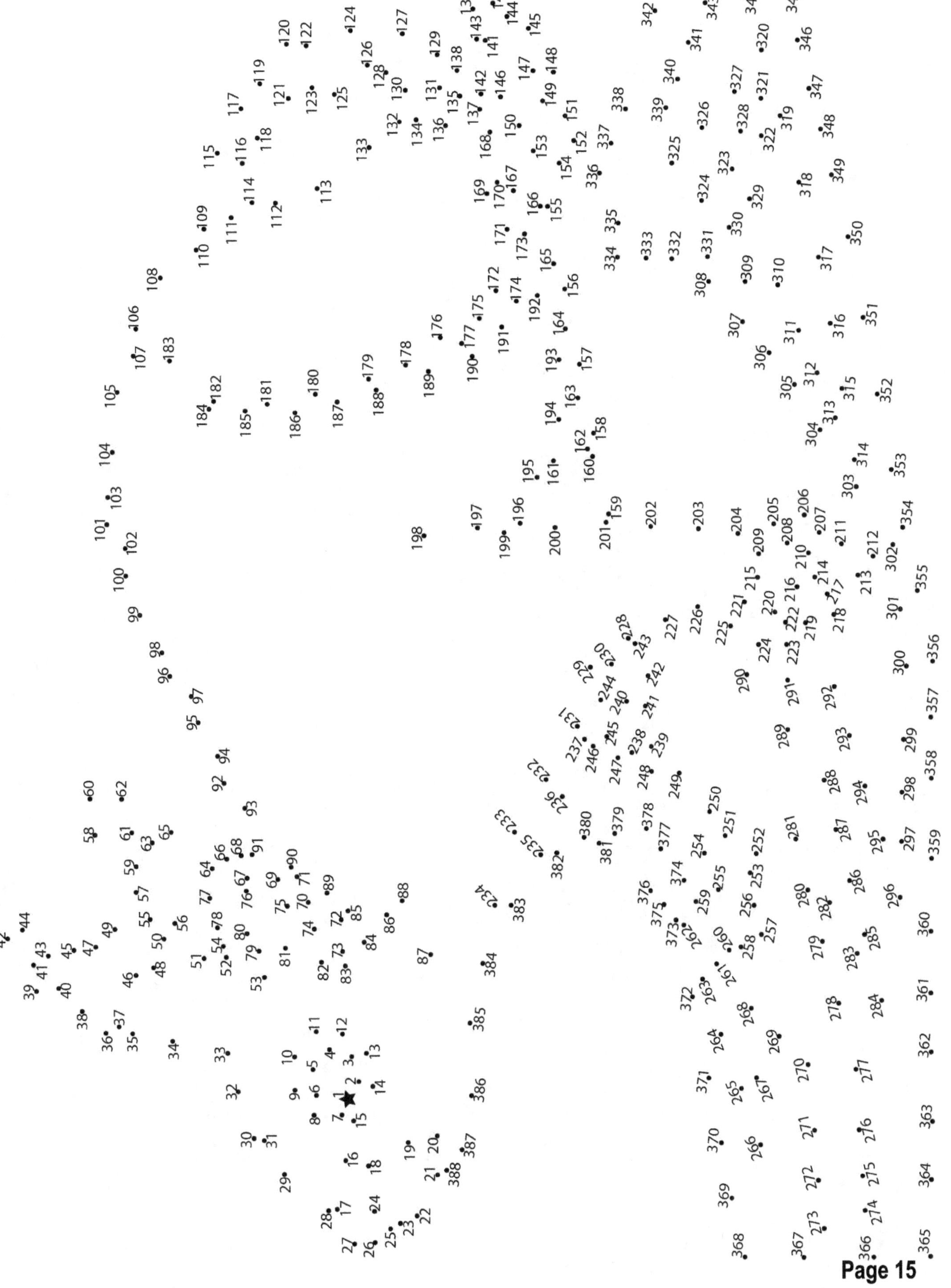

Follow along with the page numbers from top left to bottom right

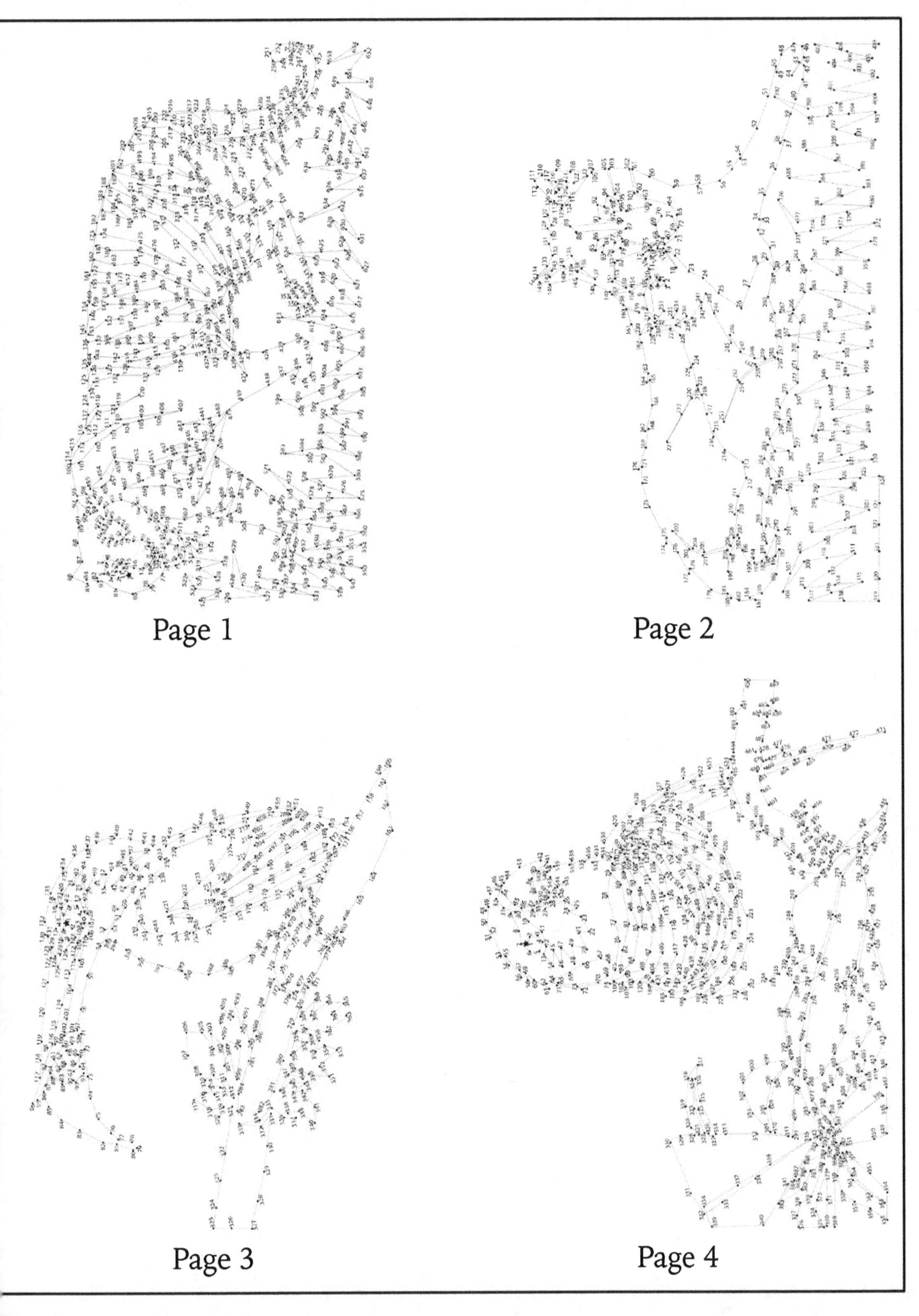

Page 1

Page 2

Page 3

Page 4

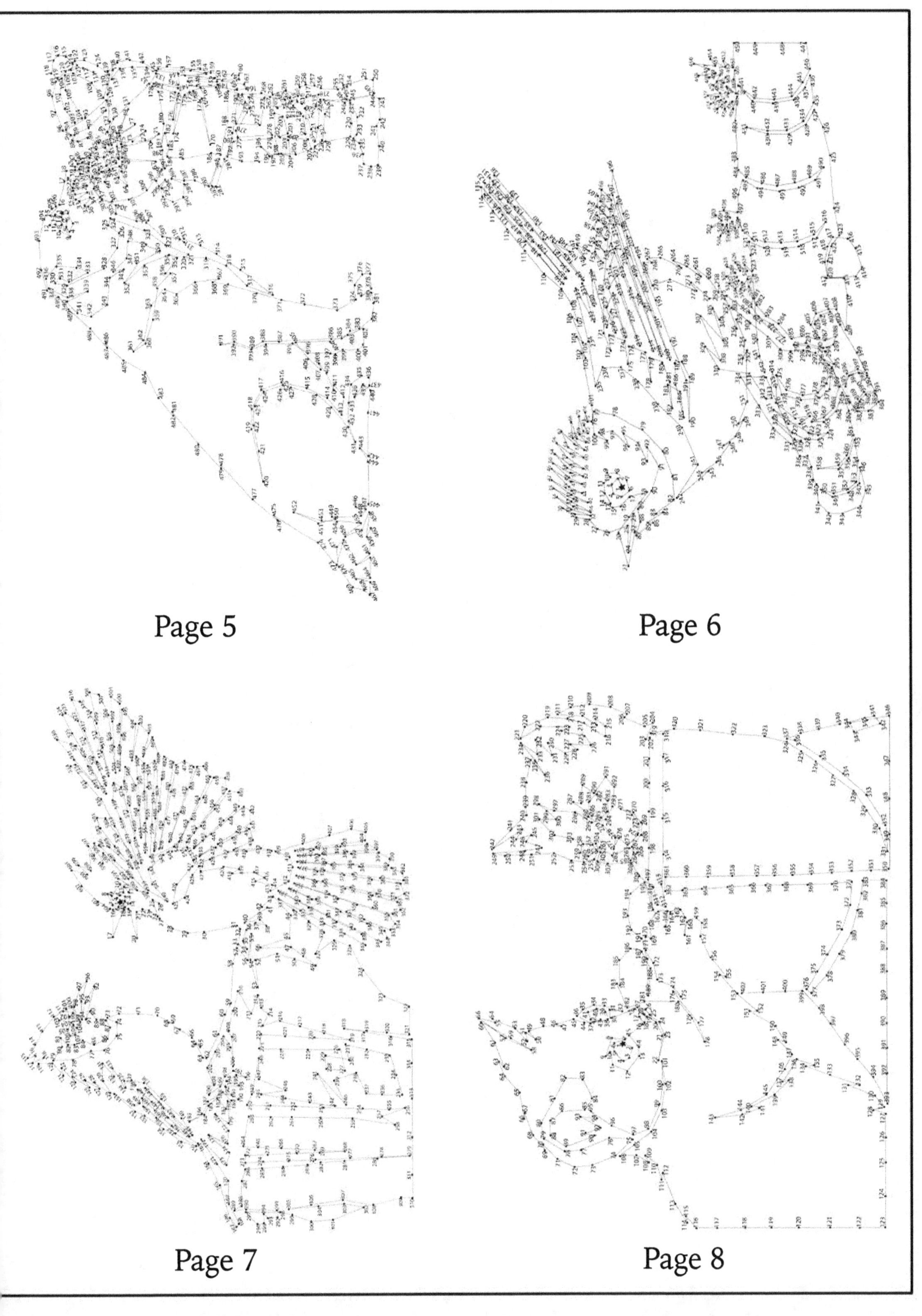

Page 5

Page 6

Page 7

Page 8

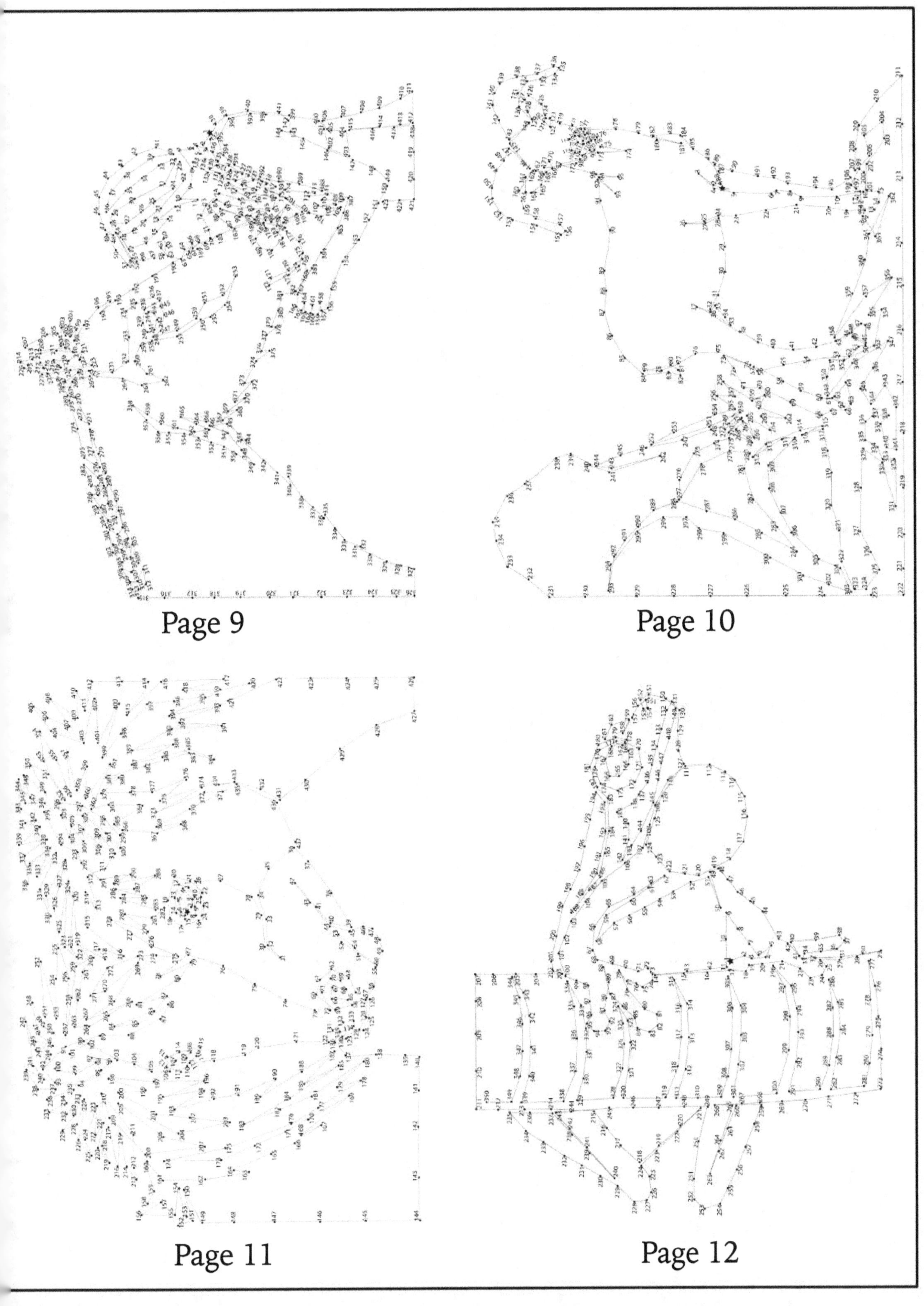

Page 9

Page 10

Page 11

Page 12

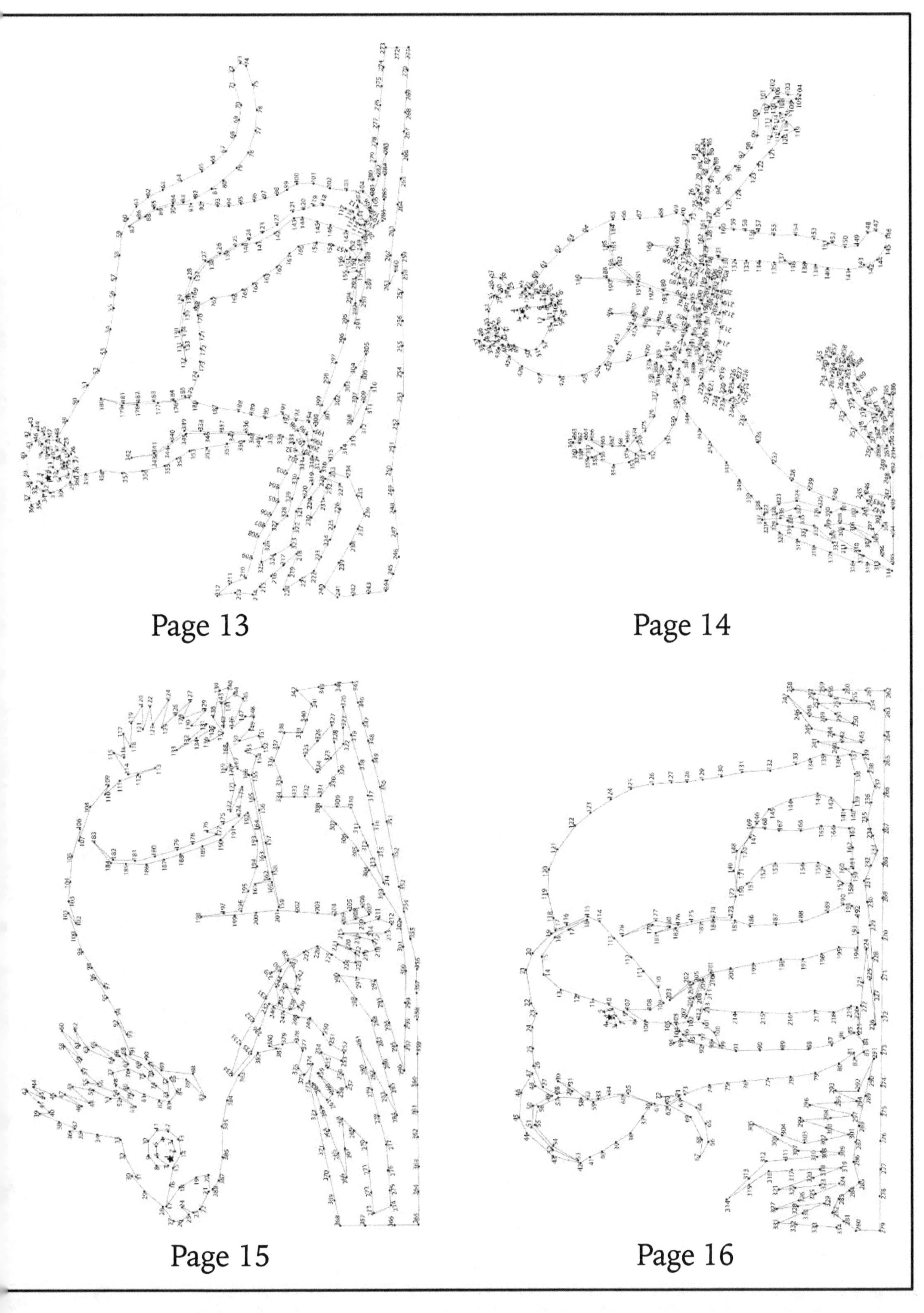

Page 13

Page 14

Page 15

Page 16

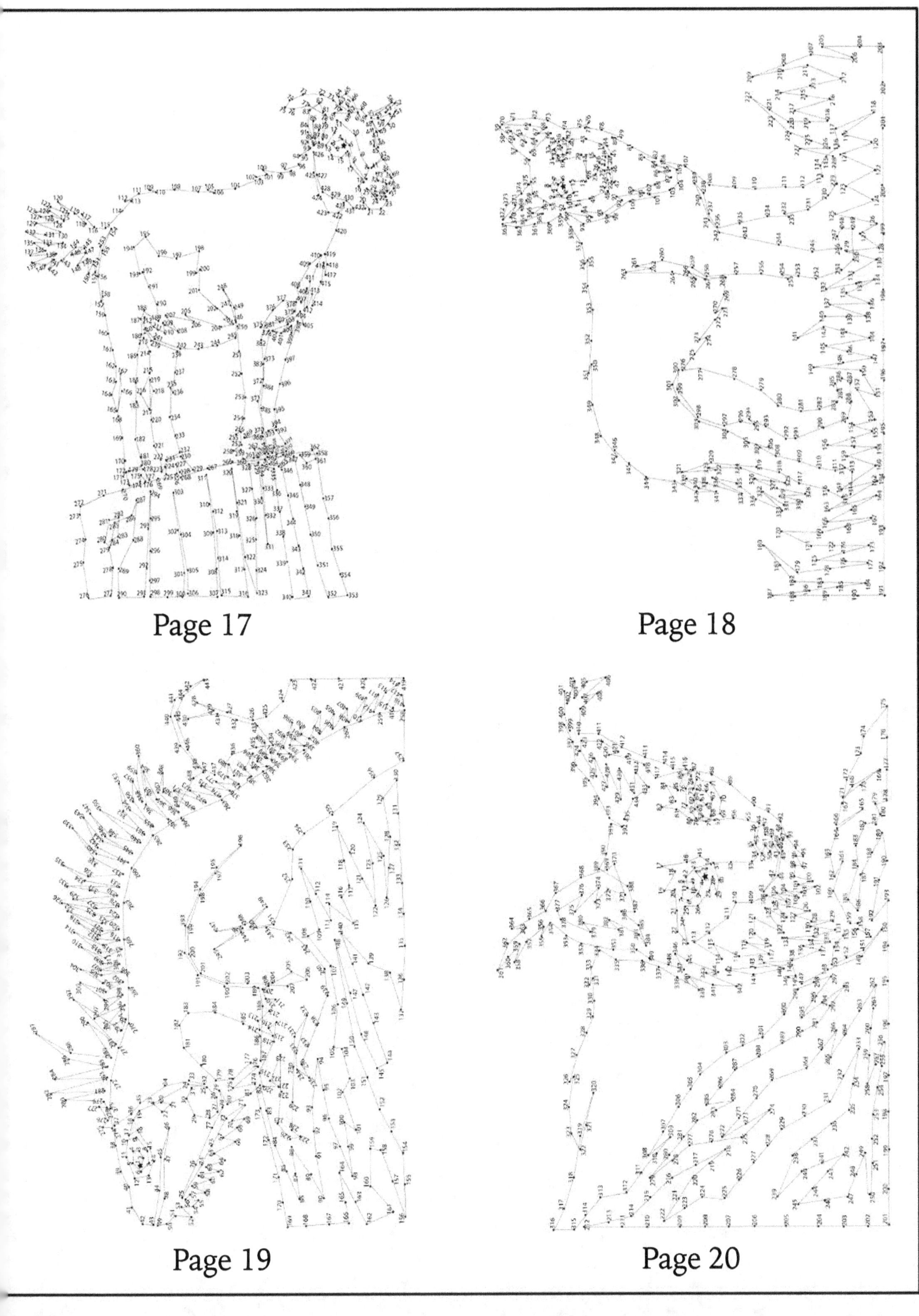

Page 17

Page 18

Page 19

Page 20

Enjoy bonus images from
some of our other fun
dot-to-dot books

Find all of our books on Amazon

Rainforest Animals and Jungle Animals
Easy to Read Large Print Dot-to-Dot
Puzzles From 150 to 600 Dots

Amazing Dogs
Large Print Dot to Dot Book For Adults
Puzzles From 150 to 760 Dots

Antique Cars And Vintage Cars
Large Print Dot-to-Dot Book For Adults
Puzzles From 150 to 610 Dots

Faye

Large Print Dot-to-Dot Sea Life
Puzzles From 150 to 433 Dots

150 151 149 148 152 147 155 146 153 154 156 145
188 187 186 174 173 175 185 172 189 190 176 184 178 177
130 129 128 127 126 136 137 144 157 171 191 183 179
131 132 133 134 135 124 125 123 138 143 158 170 192 182 180
104 103 102 120 121 122 99 98 97 139 142 159 169 181
106 105 101 119 100 88 89 90 93 95 94 96 140 141 162 163 160 168 193 195 194
107 108 112 113 118 117 87 91 92 49 48 37 35 34 161 164 196 167 166
111 116 114 115 86 73 50 44 47 36 38 33 165 197
110 109 85 74 52 51 45 46 39 32 31
75 72 53 42 41 40 30 198
82 71 54 199
84 83 77 76 70 55 56 57 29 200
81 78 69 80 68 58 28 201
79 67 284 59 27 202
285 283 66 60 12 13 26 229 203
286 288 282 11 10 9 8 14 204 228
287 290 289 281 65 61 2 3 4 7 15 25 205 206 227 207
291 280 62 18 5 6 16 21 262 261 230
292 279 64 63 17 22 23 24 265 264 266 263 226 208
278 276 275 274 273 19 20 272 268 267 320 231 260 225
293 277 271 298 318 319 233 259 209
294 270 269 317 322 321 232 234 258 224
295 296 297 316 323 235 257 210 223 211 221 212 222
299 315 324 213 220 219
300 311 312 313 236 214 215 218
310 302 314 237 238 254 256 216 217
309 303 326 342 325 239 240 255 251 241 250
308 304 341 327 328 343 346 344 252 329 340 330 338 331 251 242 249
307 305 339 332 337 243 248 244 247 245 246
333 336 306 334 335

Beautiful Flowers and Butterflies
Dot-to-Dot for Adults

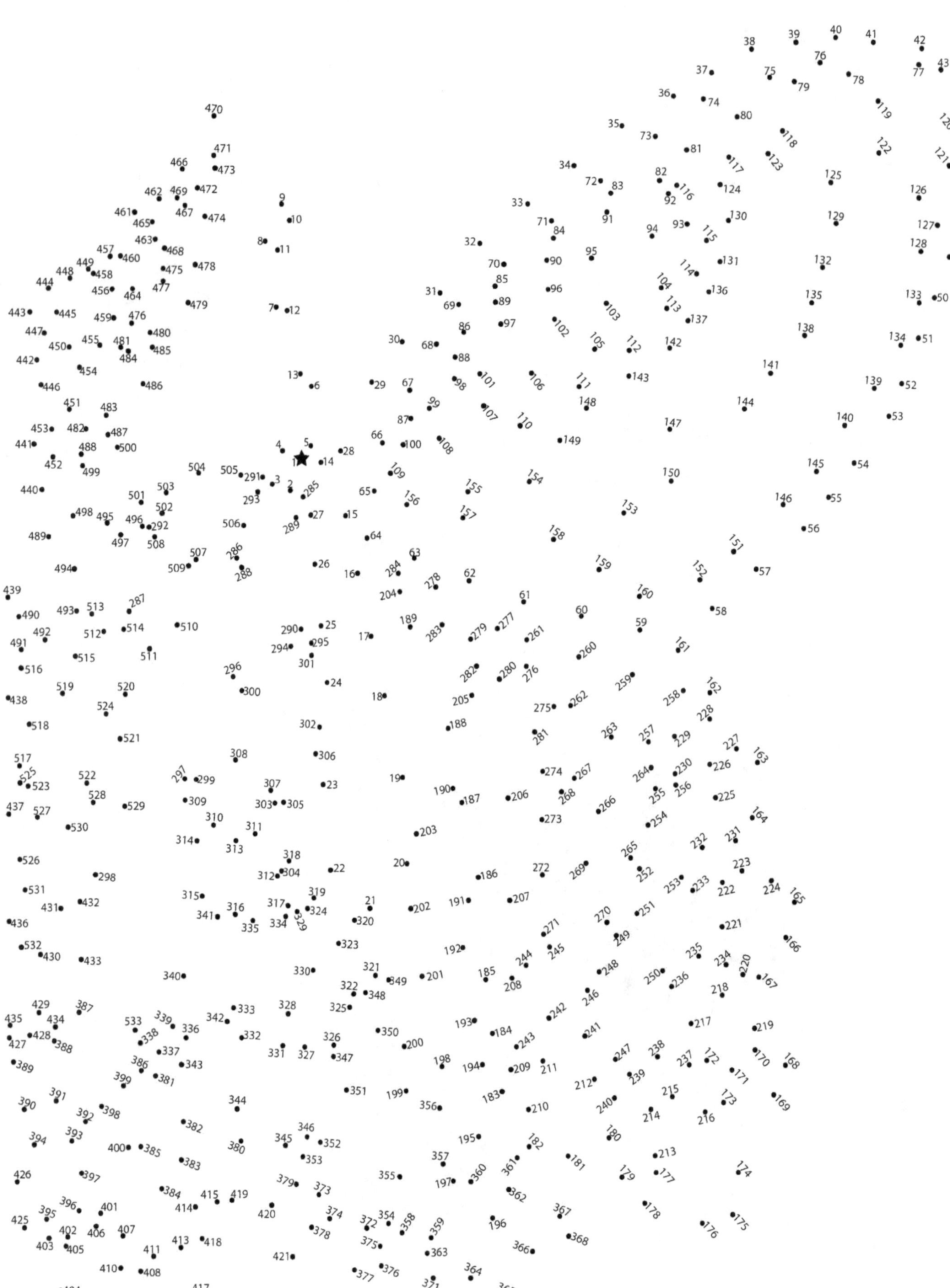

Please
Leave
Us
A Review
On Amazon